EDGE
BOOKS™

SPORTS RIVALRIES

OUTRAGEOUS

PRO FOOTBALL
RIVALRIES

BY MATT DOEDEN

CONSULTANT: CRAIG R. COENEN, PROFESSOR OF HISTORY, MERCER COUNTY COMMUNITY COLLEGE,
WEST WINDSOR, NEW JERSEY

CAPSTONE PRESS

a capstone imprint

Edge Books are published by Capstone Press,
1710 Roe Crest Drive, North Mankato, Minnesota 56003
www.capstonepub.com

Library of Congress Cataloging-in-Publication Data
Cataloging-in-publication information is on file with the Library of Congress.
ISBN 978-1-4914-2026-3 (library binding)
ISBN 978-1-4914-2197-0 (eBook PDF)

Editorial Credits
Angie Kaelberer and Alesha Sullivan, editors; Ted Williams, designer;
Eric Gohl, media researcher; Tori Abraham, production specialist

Photo Credits
AP Photo: Greg Trott, cover (top), James D Smith, cover (bottom), Paul Abell, 4–5;
CriaImages.com: Jay Robert Nash Collection, 26–27; Getty Images: Brian Bahr,
14–15, Diamond Images/Kidwiler Collection, 8–9, Rob Lindquist, 13; Newscom:
ABACAUSA.COM/Rick Wood, 1, Cal Sport Media/John Middlebrook, 28–29, EPA/
Dan Levine, 24–25, Icon SMI/Mark Cowan, 20–21, Icon SMI/Rich Kane, 16–17, Icon
SMI/Todd Kirkland, 10–11, MCT/Doug Kapustin, 22–23, MCT/Rick Wood, 6–7,
18-19

Design Elements
Shutterstock

Printed in the United States of America in Stevens Point, Wisconsin
102014   008479WZS15

Table of Contents

FIERCE COMPETITION

Few sports are as intense and hard-hitting as professional football. Hard runs, punishing tackles, and thrilling passes build excitement, both for players and fans. So it's no surprise that some of sports' most heated rivalries have sprung up in the National Football League (NFL). Some **feuds**, such as the rivalry between the Bears and the Packers, stretch back almost 100 years. But new ones, including the clash between the 49ers and the Seahawks, are always popping up. These rivalries are part of what makes the sport so much fun.

feud—a long-running quarrel between two people or groups

NFL DIVISIONS

The NFL's two conferences include eight divisions. Many of the NFL's biggest rivalries are within the divisions.

American Football Conference (AFC)

East

Buffalo Bills
Miami Dolphins
New England Patriots
New York Jets

North

Baltimore Ravens
Cincinnati Bengals
Cleveland Browns
Pittsburgh Steelers

South

Indianapolis Colts
Jacksonville Jaguars
Houston Texans
Tennessee Titans

West

Denver Broncos
Kansas City Chiefs
Oakland Raiders
San Diego Chargers

National Football Conference (NFC)

East

Dallas Cowboys
New York Giants
Philadelphia Eagles
Washington

North

Chicago Bears
Detroit Lions
Green Bay Packers
Minnesota Vikings

South

Atlanta Falcons
Carolina Panthers
New Orleans Saints
Tampa Bay Buccaneers

West

Arizona Cardinals
St. Louis Rams
San Francisco 49ers
Seattle Seahawks

The Seahawks and 49ers battle it out in a heated divisional game in 2014.

BEARS VS. PACKERS

The Chicago Bears and Green Bay Packers have been rivals since 1921. That's 188 games through the 2013 season! When the rivalry began, the Bears weren't even known as the Bears. They were the Chicago Staleys. They became the Bears the next year.

Through 2013 the Bears held the edge in the series, 93–89–6. Chicago won that first game in 1921, 20-0. Three years later a fight broke out during a 3-0 Chicago victory. Chicago's Frank Hanny and Green Bay's Tillie Voss were the first pro football players kicked out of a game for fighting. And then the battle was really on!

The rivalry was bigger than ever in 1941. They ended the season tied atop the Western Division. And so they played a third time at their first playoff meeting. The Bears came out on top, 33-14. They went on to win the NFL championship.

STATS AT A GLANCE

First Meeting:
1921 (Bears/Staleys 20, Packers 0)

All-time Series:
Bears lead 93–89–6

All-time Score:
Bears lead 3,223-3,142

Two Bears defenders gang up on Packers running back James Starks in the 2010 NFC Championship Game.

Jim Taylor (31) of the Packers tries to break the tackle of a Bears defender during a 1960s game at Lambeau field in Green Bay.

The tide turned in favor of the Packers in the 1960s. They won 15 of the 20 games that **decade**. They also won five NFL titles and the first two Super Bowls.

More recent years have also favored the Packers. Quarterbacks Brett Favre and Aaron Rodgers led Green Bay to a 32-13 record since 1992. And in the 2010 season the bitter rivals met in the playoffs for just the second time. When the Bears' quarterback Jay Cutler went out with an injury, Chicago's fate was sealed. Rodgers and the Packers won the game 21-14. They went on to win the team's fourth Super Bowl title.

WHAT'S THAT SMELL?

When the teams met for a game in 1985 the Green Bay players played a prank on the Bears. They put horse manure in their locker room! But the Bears got the last laugh. They won the game 16-10 and went on to become the Super Bowl champs that season.

—a period of 10 years

Falcons' defenders swarm toward the Saints' ball carrier Deuce McAllister in a 2006 New Orleans victory.

STATS AT A GLANCE

First Meeting:
1967 (Saints 27, Falcons 24)

All-time Series:
Falcons lead 47-43

All-time Score:
Falcons lead 1,952-1,842

SOUTHERN SHOWDOWN

New Orleans and Atlanta are both in what's called the Deep South. Some people call the area "Dixie." The close location of the cities makes the two teams perfect rivals. The first Falcons vs. Saints game in 1967 was known as the Dixie Championship. In recent years it has been called the Southern Showdown.

SAINTS VS. FALCONS

The New Orleans Saints and Atlanta Falcons first played in 1967. But their rivalry really didn't heat up until 1973. That was when the Falcons traveled to New Orleans and embarrassed the Saints 62-7.

Both teams had many losing seasons during the next 30 years. But their feud picked up steam in the 2000s. In 2005 Hurricane Katrina damaged the New Orleans Superdome. The Saints didn't play there that season. In 2006 the Saints hosted the Falcons for their first game back in New Orleans. Saints cornerback Curtis Deloatch recovered a blocked **punt** in the end zone. He scored a touchdown to help New Orleans to an emotional 23-3 win.

In December 2010 the teams battled for playoff positions on Monday Night Football. Quarterback Matt Ryan helped the Falcons build a 14-10 fourth-quarter lead. But Drew Brees led the Saints down the field for a game-winning touchdown pass. The Falcons won the division, but the Saints made the playoffs as a wild card.

punt—a play in which a punter receives the snap and kicks the ball down the field to the other team

COWBOYS
VS.
49ERS

Not all rivalries are between division foes. During much of the 1970s, 1980s, and 1990s, the rivalry between the Dallas Cowboys and San Francisco 49ers was the hottest around. They were two of the league's top teams, and they always seemed to clash. The teams met in the playoffs during the 1970, 1971, and 1972 seasons. The Cowboys won all three times.

The rivalry heated up again in 1982. The teams met in the NFC Championship. The Cowboys held a lead. But 49ers quarterback Joe Montana threw an amazing last-minute touchdown pass to wide receiver Dwight Clark to win the game. "The Catch" remains one of the most famous plays in NFL history.

The rivalry was going strong again in the 1990s. From 1993 to 1995, the teams met in three straight NFC Championships. Quarterback Troy Aikman and running back Emmitt Smith led the Cowboys to victories in 1993 and 1994. But quarterback Steve Young and the 49ers got their **revenge** in 1995. That year the 49ers went on to win Super Bowl XXIX.

revenge—an action taken in return for an injury or offense

Clark's catch led to an epic win over the Cowboys during the 1982 NFC Championship Game.

STATS AT A GLANCE

First Meeting:
1960 (49ers 26, Cowboys 14)

All-time Series:
Tied 16-16-1

All-time Score:
49ers lead 844-784

DISRESPECT

In a game in Dallas in September 2000, 49ers wide receiver Terrell Owens caught a touchdown pass. He celebrated by rushing to midfield to celebrate on the Cowboys logo, a blue star. Later in the game, "TO" caught another touchdown. He ran back to midfield to do it again. Dallas safety George Teague sprinted toward Owens and slammed him to the turf. It was proof that the rivalry was as bitter as ever.

—a visual symbol of a company or team

ONE COACH, TWO TEAMS

Coach Mike Shanahan was at the center of the Raiders/Broncos rivalry for years. In 1988 the Raiders hired Shanahan as their head coach. But he clashed with team owner Al Davis. Davis fired Shanahan early in the 1989 season. Shanahan went to the Broncos. He led them to two Super Bowl titles.

Raiders wide receiver Jerry Porter (84) celebrates after scoring a touchdown in Denver.

RAIDERS VS. BRONCOS

The Raiders and Broncos were rivals even before they joined the NFL. Their first game in 1960 was as members of the rival American Football League (AFL). The Broncos won that game 31-14. But the Raiders would **dominate** the series for the next 30 years. The AFL merged with the NFL in 1970. From 1965 to 1971, the Raiders won 14 games in a row over the Broncos. In 1978 the teams met for the first time in the playoffs. The Broncos won the game 20-17 and became the AFC champions. They lost in Super Bowl XII to Dallas.

On Monday Night Football in September 1988, the Broncos jumped to a 24-0 lead. But quarterback Jay Schroeder led the Raiders to an amazing 30-27 comeback victory.

In January 1994 the Raiders did it again. They came back from being behind by 17 points to win the game 33-30 and **clinch** a playoff spot. A week later they beat the Broncos once again in a playoff game.

In November 2004 the teams battled in a Denver snowstorm. The Broncos were set to kick the game-winning field goal late in the game. But Oakland lineman Langston Walker blocked the kick for a 25-24 victory.

dominate—to rule; in sports, a team or person dominates by winning much more than anyone else

clinch—to settle a matter once and for all

GIANTS
VS.
EAGLES

The NFC's East division is home to some of football's best rivalries. The New York Giants and the Philadelphia Eagles' feud is one of the fiercest. New York beat Philadelphia 56-0 in their first meeting in 1933. Ever since the teams have had one of the most evenly matched rivalries in the NFL.

In November 1960 the Giants and Eagles were battling for the Eastern Conference title. The Eagles led 17-10, but the Giants were driving up the field. Fullback Frank Gifford caught a short pass. As he turned to run, Eagles' linebacker Chuck Bednarik slammed into him. Gifford was knocked unconscious. He missed the rest of that season and all of the following one. "The Hit" remains one of the most famous tackles in NFL history.

In December 2010 the Giants led the Eagles 31-10 with 7:28 to play. But the Eagles charged back to tie the score. With just 12 seconds left, the Giants had to punt. Philly returner DeSean Jackson fielded the punt and ran 65 yards for the game-winning touchdown. He celebrated by tossing the ball far into the crowd.

The Philadelphia rush is on as Giants quarterback Eli Manning scans the field for an open receiver in a 2010 clash.

MIRACLE AT THE MEADOWLANDS

In a November 1978 game at the Giants' Meadowlands Sports Complex, the Giants led the Eagles 17-12. They held the ball with just 31 seconds remaining. All the Giants had to do was kneel on the ball. But they tried a handoff instead. Quarterback Joe Pisarcik and fullback Larry Csonka botched the handoff. The ball hit the ground. Eagles defensive back Herman Edwards scooped it up and ran in the winning touchdown. After the game Pisarcik needed a police escort to protect him from angry Giants fans.

STATS AT A GLANCE

First Meeting:
1933 (Giants 56, Eagles 0)

All-time Series:
Giants lead 84-76-2

All-time Score:
Giants lead 3,121-2,996

PACKERS VS. VIKINGS

Before 1961 most of Minnesota was Green Bay Packer territory. When the Vikings entered the NFL that year, a natural rivalry was born. The Packers dominated the 1960s, while the Vikings owned the 1970s. From 1992 to 2013, the teams won 16 division titles combined. The Packers won ten and the Vikings six.

The Packers won the Super Bowl in January 1997. But two seasons later, the Vikings had a new weapon, rookie wide receiver Randy Moss. On Monday Night Football in November 1998, Moss shocked the Green Bay crowd by lighting up the Packers defense. Moss gave Packer fans another reason to boo him in a 2005 playoff game. Moss pretended to pull down his pants in front of Packer fans as the Vikings beat the Packers 31-17.

The teams met in the playoffs again following the 2012 season. A week before, Minnesota had beaten Green Bay to get into the playoffs. But the Packers won 24-10 to end Minnesota's season.

STATS AT A GLANCE

First Meeting:
1961 (Packers 33, Vikings 7)

All-time Series:
Packers lead 56-49-2

All-time Score:
Packers lead 2,269-2,085

The Packers' Morgan Burnett hits the Vikings' Kyle Rudolph during an NFC wild-card playoff game at the end of the 2012 season.

BRETT FAVRE RETURNS

Quarterback Brett Favre was part of the Green Bay lineup for 16 seasons. But after the Packers went to the younger Aaron Rodgers, Favre ended up in Minnesota. In November 2009 Favre got his revenge in Green Bay, beating the Packers 38-26. Favre led the Vikings to a division title that year and nearly defeated the Saints in the conference championship.

The Colts' Joseph Addai blasts into the end zone to score the winning touchdown against the Patriots in the 2007 AFC Championship.

PATRIOTS VS. COLTS

The two dominant teams of the 2000s were the New England Patriots and the Indianapolis Colts. Their quarterbacks, Tom Brady and Peyton Manning, fueled one of the NFL's most exciting rivalries. From 2002 to 2012, the Colts and Patriots represented the AFC in the Super Bowl a combined seven times. The Patriots won three Super Bowl trophies, while the Colts won one.

Brady and the Patriots had the edge early on in the rivalry. They knocked the Colts out of the playoffs in 2004 and 2005. In 2007 the teams met for the AFC Championship. New England surged to a 21-6 halftime lead. But Manning led the Colts back in the second half, 38-34. Indianapolis running back Joseph Addai scored the game-winning touchdown.

In November 2009 the teams played one of their most interesting games. The Patriots had a 6-point lead and the ball with about two minutes left. It was fourth down with two yards to go. Most coaches would have called for a punt. But New England's coach Bill Belichick shocked everyone by going for it! The plan backfired. The Patriots didn't get the two yards, giving Manning a short field to score a touchdown. The Colts won 35-34.

STATS AT A GLANCE

First Meeting:
1970 (Colts 14, Patriots 6)

All-time Series:
Patriots lead 48-29

All-time Score:
Patriots lead 1,880-1,459

From 1950 to 1995, the Pittsburgh Steelers' biggest rival was the Cleveland Browns. But the Browns then moved to Baltimore and became the Ravens. The rivalry traveled with them and remained as hot as ever.

The Cleveland Browns' franchise returned in 1999 as an **expansion team**. They began a new rivalry with the Steelers. And of course, Cleveland fans had never forgiven the Ravens for leaving. A new three-way rivalry was born!

Pittsburgh crushed the new Browns 43-0 in their first matchup in 1999. But in the second game the Browns shocked the Steelers when Phil Dawson kicked a last-second field goal. The Browns won 16-15.

For the next 10 years, the Ravens and Steelers both dominated the AFC North division. In 2008 the Steelers beat the Ravens three times—twice during the regular season and again in the AFC Championship. In the championship game, safety Troy Polamalu intercepted a pass and returned it for a touchdown to seal a 23-14 win.

expansion team—a team added to an existing league

STATS AT A GLANCE

STEELERS VS. BROWNS

First Meeting:
1950 (Browns 30, Steelers 17)

All-time Series:
Steelers lead 67-57

All-time Score:
Steelers lead 2,533-2,389

Pittsburgh wide receiver Santonio Holmes stretches for a touchdown as the Steelers beat the Ravens in the 2008 AFC Championship showdown.

STATS AT A GLANCE

STEELERS VS. RAVENS

First Meeting:
1996 (Steelers 31, Ravens 17)

All-time Series:
Steelers lead 23-16

All-time Score:
Steelers lead 779-722

Malcom Smith comes down with an interception in the end zone to seal a Seattle victory and send them to the 2013 Super Bowl.

49ERS VS. SEAHAWKS

The hottest new rivalry in the NFL is between the San Francisco 49ers and the Seattle Seahawks. These two defensive-minded teams have dominated the NFC West in recent years.

Late in 2012 the 49ers were on their way to a division title. But on December 23, the Seahawks destroyed them 42-13. San Francisco coach Jim Harbaugh was furious. He claimed that Seattle won only because they were cheating by using banned substances.

The 49ers got their revenge a year later. This time the Seahawks were leading the division. But quarterback Colin Kaepernick led the 49ers on a game-winning drive in the final minutes.

Tension between the teams increased even more when they met in the 2013 NFC Championship game. With 22 seconds left, the 49ers were driving for the tying touchdown. But Seattle cornerback Richard Sherman deflected a Kaepernick pass to teammate Malcolm Smith. Seattle won the game 23-17. The Seahawks went on to become Super Bowl champs.

STATS AT A GLANCE

First Meeting:
1976 (49ers 37, Seahawks 21)

All-time Series:
Seahawks lead 16-15

All-time Score:
Seahawks lead 734-597

Hall of Fame quarterback Roger Staubach of the Cowboys dives for a touchdown in a 1975 matchup.

STATS AT A GLANCE

First Meeting:
1960 (Washington 26, Cowboys 14)

All-time Series:
Cowboys lead 64-42-2

All-time Score:
Cowboys lead 2,449-2,083

COWBOYS WASHINGTON

Rivalries don't get any angrier than the one between Dallas and Washington. They've played more than 100 games, with the Cowboys leading 64-42-2. But their rivalry started before they ever played a game.

The Cowboys entered the NFL in 1960 as an expansion team. Each NFL team was allowed to protect a handful of its best players. The Cowboys were then allowed to fill a roster by picking players off other teams' rosters. By mistake Washington forgot to protect Pro Bowl quarterback Eddie LeBaron. The Cowboys snagged him, and the bad feeling between the teams began.

IT'S YOUR FUNERAL

In the last game of the 1979 regular season, Dallas and Washington squared off with the division title on the line. Washington teammates sent a funeral wreath to Cowboys' defensive end Harvey Martin. Martin put it in his locker. The Cowboys beat Washington, knocking them out of the playoffs. After the game Martin stormed into the Washington locker room and threw the wreath at the opposing players.

In 1972 Washington beat the Cowboys 26-3 in their first playoff meeting. In 1979 the teams met in the season's final week for the division title. Quarterback Roger Staubach led the Cowboys to a comeback 35-34 win with two fourth-quarter touchdown drives.

In 1983 Dallas trailed Washington 24-17 in the fourth quarter of the NFC Championship. Dallas had the ball. But Washington defender Darryl Grant picked off a pass and ran it back for a touchdown.

By 2012 star quarterbacks led both teams. Dallas' Tony Romo and Washington's Robert Griffin III were two of the most exciting players in the NFL. They clashed in the last game of the 2012 season with the NFC East title on the line. Washington's running back Alfred Morris stole the show. He ran for 200 yards and 3 touchdowns to lead Washington to a 28-18 win.

LONGTIME RIVALRIES

The NFL has a long, rich history. Its rivalries run deep, and they're here to stay. As long as fans flock to the stadiums on game day, players will be pumped up to defeat their rivals and become champions.

Washington running back Alfred Morris tries to break a tackle in a 2012 contest against Dallas.

Glossary

clinch (KLINCH)—to settle a matter once and for all

decade (DEK-ayd)—a period of 10 years

dominate (DAH-muh-nayt)—to rule; in sports, a team or person dominates by winning much more than anyone else

expansion team (ik-SPAHN-shuhn TEEM)—a team added to an existing league

feud (FYOOD)—a long-running quarrel between two people or groups of people

logo (LOH-goh)—a visual symbol of a company or team

punt (PUHNT)—a play in which a punter receives the snap and kicks the ball down the field to the other team

revenge (rih-VENJ)—an action taken in return for an injury or offense

Read More

Hetrick, Hans. *The Super Bowl: All about Pro Football's Biggest Event.* Winner Takes All. North Mankato, Minn.: Capstone Press, 2013.

Hurley, Michael. *Football.* Fantastic Sports Facts. Chicago: Capstone Raintree, 2013.

Rausch, David. *National Football League.* Epic: Major League Sports. Minneapolis: Bellwether Media, 2014.

Internet Sites

FactHound offers a safe, fun way to find Internet sites related to this book. All of the sites on FactHound have been researched by our staff.

Here's all you do:

Visit *www.facthound.com*

Type in this code: 9781491420263

Super-cool stuff! Check out projects, games and lots more at **www.capstonekids.com**

Index